IGNITE! Leadership Transformation

Be The Leader They Remember

By Timothy MK

Table of Contents

Introduction

Becoming an exceptional leader necessitates cultivating a unique blend of capabilities, including fostering trust, exuding reliability, and honing communication aptitude. It also entails possessing the capacity to motivate and continuously develop one's leadership abilities. This book aims to furnish you with ten invaluable strategies that can amplify your leadership prowess, empowering you to excel in diverse roles, whether as a CEO, manager, coach, or any leadership position.

Leadership transcends the mere completion of tasks. It involves igniting passion in your team and synergizing collective efforts toward the actualization of a shared vision. The key to extraordinary leadership lies in consistently communicating an inspiring vision of the future, thereby motivating others to align their actions accordingly. It is this talent for compelling communication and visionary thinking that distinguishes exemplary leaders.

Great leaders not only concentrate on task completion but also ensure their team comprehends the purpose and significance behind those tasks. Enthusiasm is infectious, and an enthusiastic team leads to enhanced performance.

This book provides actionable techniques to help you foster enthusiasm, listen attentively, develop self awareness, control emotions, communicate expectations clearly, build trust through empowerment, influence skillfully, adapt your leadership style, deliver candid feedback, and embrace feedback. Equipped with these strategies, you can elevate your leadership abilities and create an environment where individuals feel empowered to excel. Let us explore the depths of leadership excellence.

Chapter 1 Enthusiasm & Passion - A Powerful Combination

Outstanding leaders recognize that their role transcends merely overseeing the execution of tasks and projects. Truly exceptional leaders have mastered the art of igniting genuine enthusiasm and passion within their team members. They exude authentic excitement and bring infectious energy to their work.

A leader's success and influence does not solely hinge on their capabilities, technical skills, or level of experience. While these are important factors, what truly differentiates extraordinary leaders is their flair for communicating an inspiring vision that motivates others. They have a natural talent for sharing future goals and plans in a compelling manner that aligns and energizes their team.

Legendary leaders throughout history like Mahatma Gandhi, Martin Luther King Jr., and Nelson Mandela did not rise to prominence merely through skills or qualifications. Rather, it was their ability to articulate a vivid vision of the future and rally others behind their mission that allowed them to drive monumental change.

Their enthusiasm and passion for their causes was infectious and inspired action across continents.

Great leaders recognize that their fundamental duty involves more than driving task completion and micromanaging operations. Their primary responsibility lies in ensuring that every team member fully comprehends the deeper purpose and meaning behind all tasks and projects undertaken.

When leaders take the time and effort to explain why a particular project matters and how it fits into the organization's broader mission and goals, it provides helpful context. This clarity of purpose ignites engagement, enhances workplace meaning and fulfillment, and fuels productivity.

Every organization, whether a Fortune 500 company, nonprofit entity, sports team, or student club, has a central mission and purpose for existing. While each employee and team member may understand generally what the organization does, many are unaware of how their individual roles contribute to that larger purpose.

For instance, an accountant at an environmental nonprofit may believe that only the scientists, researchers, and public policy experts directly aid the mission by developing green technologies and lobbying for ecological regulations. However, an effective leader would explain how diligent financial tracking, reporting, and auditing helps maximize the impact of every dollar that the nonprofit spends. This enables the accountant to see that they are playing an integral role in furthering the organization's vision.

Enthusiasm is contagious. A team with high energy and passion for the collective cause they are working towards has been shown to outperform teams lacking engagement and meaning. Workers who believe their labor has purpose and impact produce higher quality work compared to those just doing it for a paycheck.

Leaders who fail to articulate why an individual's or team's contributions matter are squandering a massive opportunity for engagement. When team members feel that their efforts lead to something more significant than just producing widgets or increasing revenue, they often begin to display enhanced enthusiasm, dedication, and performance.

Here are some techniques that outstanding leaders deploy to cultivate genuine enthusiasm and passion within their teams:

Communicate the Big Picture Vision

Effective leaders recognize the importance of repetitive communication when attempting to imprint the organization's central vision and goals into the minds of each employee. They seize every appropriate opportunity in meetings, presentations, emails, and casual conversation to reinforce how various projects and tasks align with the broader strategic aims.

Rather than keeping the grand vision locked away in their mind or assuming everyone already grasps it, exemplary leaders err on the side of overcommunication. They reiterate the big picture vision and tie it back constantly to the individual and team work being done. This continual reinforcement ensures it remains top of mind.

When communicating the overarching vision, great leaders express it simply and vividly. They know that complex, convoluted explanations will fail to spark enthusiasm. Using clear language, memorable analogies, and real world examples helps crystallize the vision for each team member.

Celebrate Milestones

On the journey toward lofty goals, teams will reach various milestones along the way. Both major and minor milestones present golden opportunities for leaders to reinforce enthusiasm and positivity.

Commemorate milestone achievements by highlighting them in meetings, sending congratulatory emails, and displaying visual tokens of progress to keep momentum high. Take the time to explain exactly how reaching the milestone gets the team closer towards actualizing the broader mission.

Celebrations keep spirits high and allow teams to appreciate how much they have already accomplished on the path to ambitious goals. Marking milestones provides a series of encouraging boosts that build team confidence and optimism as they tackle the next phase.

Encourage Creative Input

Leaders can supercharge enthusiasm by encouraging teams to actively participate in shaping the vision and determining how to bring it to life most effectively.

Rather than solely issuing rigid decrees from the top down, outstanding leaders regularly ask for input and creative suggestions from the team members tasked with executing the vision. This empowers individuals and makes them feel deeply invested in driving the mission forward collaboratively.

Brainstorming sessions are excellent ways to spur creative thinking. When people see their own ideas validated and implemented, it amplifies their sense of purpose and ownership. Welcome wild and unconventional suggestions, as these often produce the greatest innovations. Fostering a collaborative, creative environment spurs the enthusiasm that unlocks team potential.

Convey Confidence

Enthusiasm thrives when leaders clearly communicate confidence in their team's abilities and potential to achieve collective goals. Highlight past shared accomplishments as proof of what you can achieve together.

Setting bold, ambitious goals is thrilling but can also seem daunting at the onset. Self Doubt might creep in and extinguish the initial sparks of enthusiasm. This makes confidence boosting by the leader critical.

Great leaders recognize when teams need reassurance and inspiration to sustain their excitement. They remind the group of their relevant skills, strengths, and talents that make them qualified to accomplish their objectives. When individuals feel genuinely respected and valued for their expertise, their enthusiasm is rekindled.

Model Engagement

The most vital way for leaders to cultivate sincere enthusiasm is to model it constantly in their own actions. Leading by example is the only authentic way to inspire passion across an organization.

When leaders visibly display enthusiasm in their interactions with teams, it rapidly cascades down through the ranks. Even seemingly trivial actions like maintaining a cheerful disposition, speaking positively about projects, and expressing interest in individuals' roles can snowball into widespread engagement when consistently modeled.

Conversely, nothing snuffs out enthusiasm faster than leaders who stay disengaged. Team members notice when leaders seem distracted, disinterested or negative and it directly stifles their motivation. By setting the tone at the top with their own behavior, leaders possess tremendous power to shape organizational culture.

Make it Fun

Hard work and fun are not mutually exclusive. Outstanding leaders recognize that incorporating playfulness and lightheartedness into the workplace keeps energy and spirits high.

Pursuing ambitious goals often requires teams to put in long hours and high intensity mental focus. However, leaders should intersperse periods of fun downtime to provide a release valve and prevent burnout.

Organizing team outings, celebrating birthdays, encouraging workplace friendships, and infusing humor into meetings are all simple ways leaders can foster enjoyment. The most effective leaders understand that fun is a key ingredient for sustaining long term enthusiasm.

Address Enthusiasm Barriers

Of course, even in a highly motivated team, there may be some individuals who struggle to display the same level of enthusiasm and passion for the shared mission.

Leaders must uncover the reasons for this disengagement and address them. Common barriers like insufficient skills, lack of role clarity, inadequate tools, or interpersonal conflicts must be swiftly rectified before they can metastasize into teamwide morale issues.

Engaging resistant individuals in candid one on one conversations to understand their concerns is the first step. Demonstrating that their viewpoint is valued, despite differing from the consensus, helps gradually build buyin. With active listening and guidance, leaders can eventually convert even skepticism into enthusiasm.

Enthusiasm That Endures

Cultivating enduring enthusiasm requires much more than pep talks, slogans, and buzzwords. Real passion is activated when leaders invest time to explain the deeper purpose driving the work, celebrate incremental progress, solicit creative input, express confidence, lead by example, foster fun, and address barriers.

By dedicating themselves to enthusiastically communicating vision and meaning, exceptional leaders inspire their teams to give 100% of their potential each day. For leaders looking to drive change and propel their organization to the next level, genuine enthusiasm is the indispensable fuel.

Chapter 2 Shut Up and Listen

Being heard and understood is a fundamental human need. When leaders make the effort to actively listen and validate their team members' perspectives, it builds trust, fosters inclusivity, and strengthens relationships. Leaders who listen effectively are far more likely to inspire engagement and unlock the potential of their people.

Yet despite its immense benefits, skillful listening remains an underutilized tool in most leaders' repertoires. In our fast paced, digital age where distractions abound, giving someone your full, undivided attention has become a rare gift. Practicing attentive listening requires patience, focus, and intentionality but rewards you with deeper mutual understanding and connection.

Core Elements of Active Listening

What does active listening involve? More than just passively hearing words spoken, effective listening entails engaging all your senses to fully absorb the speaker's message and intended meaning. Core elements include:

- Focused Attention: Give your complete, undistracted concentration. Eliminate external distractions and inner mental chatter. Maintain eye contact without frequently glancing elsewhere. Truly listen with your entire mind and body.
- Reflective Paraphrasing: Restate the essence of what the person communicated to confirm your understanding. Phrases like "What I'm hearing is..." are helpful.
- Thoughtful Questioning: Ask smart, open ended questions that elicit deeper details and insights. Inquiries that start with "what", "how", "why" or "tell me more" prompt elaboration.
- NonVerbal Cues: Pay attention to body language, facial expressions, and tone of voice that provide subtle context beyond the words themselves. Posture, gestures, and reactions help convey meaning.
- Empathetic Mirroring: Attempt to understand the person's perspective by putting yourself in their position. Imagine how you might feel or respond in their shoes.
- Minimal Interruption: Avoid interjecting your own stories or opinions. Let the speaker share fully before responding. Refrain from finishing their sentences.

Being fully present in the moment with someone demonstrates that you consider them worthy of your time and attention. When you listen deeply, free of multitasking or mental wandering, people sense your sincerity. This validation builds trust and connection.

Listen More Than You Speak

As Stephen Covey wrote in The 7 Habits of Highly Effective People, "Most people do not listen with the intent to understand; they listen with the intent to reply." This tendency encumbers meaningful communication. Actively controlling your natural urge to share immediate reactions requires conscious effort.

Ask yourself: "Am I listening to understand this person? Or merely to prepare my response?" The latter approach short circuits the listening process. As the leader, make the exchanges more about drawing out others than stating your opinions. Your insights will resonate greater when rooted in a place of mutual comprehension.

Hone Your Questioning Skills

- Well Crafted, thoughtful questions demonstrate your genuine interest in the speaker's viewpoint and experiences. Expanding your repertoire of strategic inquiries will enrich every conversation:

- Open Ended questions that start with what, why, how, or tell me provoke deeper thought. For example: "What drew you to this profession?"
- Clarifying questions help resolve confusion. "Could you provide an example of what you mean?"
- "And" questions build on previous comments. "You mentioned the project scope was unclear. And how did that affect the timeline?"
- Empowerment questions inspire solutions. "In an ideal scenario, what do you think the strategy should be?"
- Values questions reveal motivations. "What matters most to you in this situation?"

Strategic use of probing questions spotlights nuances and drives greater mutual comprehension. Mastering this skill magnifies your active listening prowess.

Read NonVerbal Cues

Look beyond the literal words someone communicates. Their nonverbal signals often reveal valuable insights.

Facial expressions indicating confusion, frustration, or displeasure strongly color the meaning of spoken phrases. A clenched jaw or furrowed brow suggests disagreement, even if the words sound supportive. Leaders attuned to body language access a secondary layer of communication.

Likewise, notice changes in vocal tone, pace, and volume. Statements delivered in an angry shout or sarcastic drawl impart very different connotations versus a calm, thoughtful cadence. Listen between the lines.

When verbal and nonverbal messages diverge, address it explicitly. "You just mentioned being comfortable with the timeline, but your expression suggests otherwise. Help me understand your concerns." Clarifying mixed signals proactively fosters candid dialogue.

Demonstrate Empathy

While actively listening, imagine yourself in the other person's circumstances. How might the situation look through their eyes? What emotions might they be feeling? By temporarily adopting their perspective, you cultivate empathy.

Repeating someone's own words back to them and commenting on emotions evident lets them know you are striving to comprehend their vantage point. Even without fully agreeing, demonstrating empathy around differences can be powerful.

No one wants to feel alone. When leaders listen with empathy, teams feel safe enough to express vulnerability and resolve issues constructively.

While improving active listening skills takes effort, common detrimental habits must also be intentionally avoided. Some pitfalls to avoid include:

- Interrupting or talking over people.
- Downplaying others' concerns as trivial.
- Letting the mind wander. Eyes glaze over.
- Dismissing nonverbal cues and body language.
- Judging or prematurely evaluating ideas.
- Planning responses rather than listening fully.
- Hearing without making sense of meaning.
- Projecting your own assumptions onto the speaker.
- Listening for facts rather than emotions and feelings.

Catch yourself mid conversation if you slip into these patterns, make amends, and course correct. Over time, remaining present becomes second nature.

Listen Actively in Groups

Leaders often engage with team members in group settings like meetings and brainstorms. This complicates active listening, since you cannot solely focus on one speaker. Strive to:

- Maintain eye contact with whoever is speaking. Avoid side conversations.

- Paraphrase group sentiments: "What I'm hearing many of you express is..."
- Invite quieter members to share perspectives. Draw them out with questions.
- Clarify any vague or conflicting messages from the group.
- Park interesting side topics in a "parking lot" document to revisit later.
- Prevent dominant talkers from commandeering the dialogue.

Though demanding, group listening done well ensures everyone feels heard. This builds collective alignment, trust, and inclusive decision making.

Listen Even in Disagreement

When someone communicates opinions or ideas you disagree with, it can short circuit your ability to listen attentively. You may become preoccupied with formulating counter arguments. However, even in disagreement, focus first on comprehension:

- Note areas of alignment before addressing differences. Build common ground.
- Ask questions to elicit the reasoning behind their perspective. Understand their motivations.
- Maintain composure even if emotions run high. Do not get defensive.
- Look for merits in their position, even if flawed. Find truth amid falsehoods.

- Clarify how this disagreement might stem from different priorities and values.

While complex conversations may not end in perfect accord, the other person will walk away feeling respected and heard when you truly listen. Keep communicating, even across divides.

Listen to Learn

Cultivating your active listening abilities requires commitment and conscious effort. You must firmly decide to become a learner, elevate other perspectives above your own, and understand individuals profoundly. Listening intently to connect, not just react, vastly enriches communication.

By embracing attentive listening as a leader, your team members will feel valued, understood, and motivated to engage. Hone these skills and make it a cornerstone of your leadership style.

When coworkers realize that their leader authentically listens and cares about their viewpoints, it powerfully catalyzes organizational trust and unity. Mastering the art of attentive listening helps transform work relationships from mere transactions to deeper human connections.

Chapter 3 Know Yourself - Being Self Aware

"Know thyself." This ancient Greek aphorism encapsulates the immense value of self awareness for leadership growth. When you devote time to genuinely understanding your innate strengths, blind spots, biases, and triggers, you equip yourself to lead effectively and relate empathetically. Self Aware leaders act with authenticity and purpose.

Lacking self knowledge severely hampers your ability to guide others. How can you assist teammates in overcoming their limitations if unaware of your own? Or optimize team dynamics without grasping your ingrained tendencies? Becoming a superior leader necessitates the courage to honestly confront your inner landscape.

Exemplary leaders recognize that self awareness is a lifelong endeavor rather than a one time event. They embrace regular self examination and feedback to continually refine their leadership approach. Even if humbling or uncomfortable, seeking truth about yourself is the only pathway to reach your leadership potential.

Benefits of Growing Self Awareness

Intentionally developing your self awareness provides many advantages:

- Making better decisions aligned with your values
- Identifying capabilities to leverage and weaknesses to improve
- Understanding how your personality positively and negatively impacts others
- Increasing your authenticity and emotional intelligence
- Becoming more receptive to diverse perspectives and new ideas
- Pinpointing unproductive patterns of behavior or thought
- Recognizing biases so they do not undermine judgment
- Adapting your style to motivate different personalities
- Building stronger relationships rooted in trust

Without looking inward, none of this growth is possible. Self Awareness fuels all other improvements.

Techniques to Build SelfAwareness

How can leaders cultivate more insightful self perception?

- Seek feedback: Ask colleagues for candid observations on your leadership style, communication, and influence. Be open to harsh truths.

- Keep a journal: Journal regularly about situations, reactions, conversations. Review entries to find themes.
- Reflect on experiences: After events and conversations, reflect on what went well or poorly. Identify lessons.
- Take personality assessments: Complete tests like MyersBriggs, DISC, or Enneagram to better understand your traits.
- Examine your triggers: Note situations that consistently provoke strong emotions like anger or defensiveness.
- Ask "why?": When making major decisions, discuss why you made that choice to identify motivations.
- Consider alternate perspectives: See issues from different angles. How would someone else evaluate this situation?
- Admit your flaws: Be honest about weaknesses and mistakes. Take responsibility rather than blaming external factors.

These methods reveal insight, but require courage and brutal self honesty regarding who you are. Avoid superficial assessments by digging deep.

Reflect on Biases

All people harbor unconscious biases that silently skew their judgments. These may include:

- Anchoring bias: First impressions overly color future perceptions.
- Confirmation bias: Preferentially noticing validating information. Discounting contrary evidence.
- Ingroup bias: Favoring members of your own groups over outsiders.
- Halo effect: Generalizing one positive trait into a global positive perception.
- Conservatism: Resistance to change ideas, systems, or worldviews.Bringing biases to light minimizes their influence.
- Recognition error: Mistaking one person for another based on implicit associations.
- Attribution bias: Inferring people's behavior to innate traits rather than external factors.
- Conformity bias: Tendency to adopt viewpoints perceived as majority opinion.

Uncovering your biases enables you to pinpoint areas requiring growth. Strive to judge people and situations objectively.

Grow Through Discomfort

Developing self awareness pushes you outside comfort zones. The temptation to avoid scrutiny and stick with familiar self perception is natural. However, embracing discomfort leads to exponential leadership growth.

Receiving harsh feedback can sting, but do not become defensive. Get curious about the kernels of truth. Even seemingly unfair criticism likely contains some validity if you reflect openly.

Resist simply justifying your flaws and biases as permanent and unchangeable. With courage and determination, self awareness can be transformed into self improvement. Each incremental step compounds.

By committing to the lifelong adventure of discovering your true self – strengths, flaws, blind spots and all – you open the door to your highest leadership potential. Your example will inspire others to embark on the same journey.

Chapter 4 Mastering Emotions

Amid the swirling chaos that leaders routinely face, maintaining composure represents a vital capability. When confronted with criticism, setbacks, and conflict, the temptation to react emotionally presents itself. Anger, frustration, and defensiveness are natural human responses to threats and uncertainty. However, masterful leaders stay grounded in reason and equip themselves to respond constructively. Harnessing your emotions enables you to apply all your faculties effectively to the situation at hand.

The capacity to regulate your emotional state and handle adversity with calm poise conveys confidence and garners respect. Teams instinctively turn to steady minded leaders during times of upheaval and crisis. Your demeanor sets the tone. By modeling emotional balance and resilience, you help others find their center as well.

Cultivating emotional mastery does not imply suppressing authentic feelings or projecting an artificial aura of stoicism. Skilled leaders appropriately display vulnerability, passion, and sensitivity balanced by the ability to avoid reactive outbursts. Your emotions may still run strong, but you prudently choose when to reveal them strategically rather than reflexively. This emotional intelligence allows you to navigate challenges skillfully.

The Perils of Mismanaged Emotions

What happens when leaders fail to develop emotional self regulation? The consequences can be severe:

- Reactive decisions driven by impulse rather than logic
- Harsh overreactions that breed resentment and erode trust
- Negative role modeling that spreads reactive behaviors through the organization
- Escalation of highly charged situations due to lack of composure
- Inadvertent revealing of vulnerabilities better kept private
- Statements you later come to regret spoken out of anger
- Lack of reliability during crises when composure is paramount

By giving your uncontrolled emotions free rein, you cede power to base impulses over higher order reasoning and intuition. Skilled leaders domesticate their emotions without crushing them.

Techniques to Regulate Emotions

So how can leaders build their capacity to maintain composure during turbulent events?

- Take a timeout: When provoked, take a break to calm down before responding. Even a short walk helps. Do not act rashly.
- Seek counsel: Talk to trusted mentors and advisors to gain more objective insights on the situation. New perspectives defuse reactive tendencies.
- Practice mindfulness: When strong emotions arise, pause and bring your attention fully into the present moment. Observe your thoughts and physical sensations nonjudgmentally as they pass through your mind and body. Return your focus to your breathing.
- Reflect afterward: After intense moments have passed, reflect rationally on what happened once emotions have settled. Identify lessons and pinpoint overreactions.
- Get rest: Ensure adequate sleep, nutrition, and renewal activities so you have the physical and mental reserves to handle distress without burnout exacerbating volatility.
- Exercise and move: Release angry energy through non harmful physical activities like cardio, strength training, yoga, walks in nature. Don't direct frustration at other people.
- Find meaning: Even in failure and trauma, actively search for growth opportunities. Derive strength from adversity by ascribing it higher meaning.

By diligently developing these habits, you retain power over your emotions rather than allowing them to control you. Mastery arrives through consistent practice. With time, retaining clear composure during turmoil becomes second nature.

Cultivate Emotional Intelligence

Expanding your emotional intelligence represents a pivotal facet of maintaining mastery over your feelings. Emotionally intelligent leaders can accurately identify the emotions within themselves and others based on subtleties. They comprehend how emotive states impact thinking and actions. This enables them to respond empathetically and influence individuals based on emotional cues vs. just words or incentives.

Ways to elevate your emotional intelligence include:
- Carefully observe body language and nonverbal signals. Pay attention to facial microexpressions, gestures, and posture that reveal suppressed emotions.
- Listen to the tone of voice. Vocal cues like volume, speed, tremors, and inflection communicate emotional context beyond the literal words spoken.

- Discuss feelings candidly. Foster open environments where people feel safe directly sharing emotions rather than masking them.
- Sit with discomfort. Resist the urge to suppress difficult emotions like fear, sadness, hurt, anger. Allow yourself to fully experience them first.
- Identify your own stress responses. Become sharply aware of your tendencies when under duress so you can catch reactive patterns early.
- Empathize, don't just sympathize. Strive to deeply understand teammates' realities, challenges, motivations, and emotions beyond surface level.
- Provide emotional support. When others express difficult emotions, demonstrate understanding through active listening, validation, and compassion.

By strengthening emotional awareness and empathy, leaders can forge deeper connections with colleagues and provide guidance tailored to individuals' emotional landscapes. These skills compound exponential returns over time.

Convert Anger into Positive Change

As a leader, anger often arises when expectations go unmet, trust is breached, or unethical behavior occurs. Leaders who care deeply feel angry when things they value are threatened. While anger has value in alerting you to issues requiring address, unchecked anger breeds resentment, clouds rationality, and hurts people unfairly if unleashed carelessly.

Rather than seeking to suppress anger, adopt techniques to direct it toward constructive ends:

- Identify the roots: Dig beneath the surface when angry. Understand specifically what issues triggered this response in you. Get granular about what you feel was unfair or harmful.
- Allow time to process: Give yourself space for the initial intensity of the anger to fade before discussing the issue with others. Don't act instantly.
- Find common ground: In conflict, identify shared goals, needs, and motivations with the person you are angry with. Anger thrives on division. Build bridges.
- Convert anger into positive action: Redirect your angry energy into calmly fixing underlying structural problems and behaviors. Avoid attacking people.
- Forgive: Once underlying issues have been meaningfully addressed, consciously release any lingering resentment. Holding onto anger long term remains corrosive.

⊠   Use rituals: Some people find cathartic value in
      rituals like writing unsent letters or burning
      mementos of the hurt as symbolic closure.

The key is funneling anger into constructive dialogue
and initiative rather than uncontrolled venting. Modeling
healthy anger management establishes boundaries
while allowing room for redemption. Productive change
can emerge when leaders transform raw anger into
reformative purpose.

Stand Strong in Your Values

A major source of anger arises when leaders perceive
something they value to be under attack, like honesty,
excellence, accountability, diversity, or impartiality. Their
anger stems from righteous indignation.

However, those values must still be defended with
emotional discipline, not reactive outbursts. Stand firm
in your principles, but wield them with responsible
grace. Righteous anger must be channeled like any
other form.

By cultivating comprehensive emotional mastery, you
gain freedom from volatility. Meet uncertainty with
grounded equanimity and adversities with grace under
pressure. Your calm presence of mind unlocks your
leadership potential. Follow the maxim: "Be angry but do

not sin; do not let the sun go down on your anger."
Master your emotions, and they will fuel instead of fetter
you.

Chapter 5 Be Clear! Be Clear! Be Clear!

When leaders fail to communicate expectations, priorities, and success metrics clearly, confusion and frustration fester. Conversely, when leaders are explicit regarding goals, strategies, roles, and evaluation criteria, teams can align their efforts efficiently. Articulating desired outcomes clearly is a vastly underappreciated leadership skill.

Many leaders assume that staff intrinsically grasp institutional goals and plans. In reality, strategic priorities often become diluted or misinterpreted as they cascade down the hierarchy. Moreover, leaders themselves may only be loosely aligned on direction. Establishing crystalline clarity at all levels concentrates purpose and coordination.

Beyond just stating expectations, outstanding leaders ensure everyone comprehends their responsibilities through active listening, inviting questions, and providing helpful context. This lucidity creates empowerment. When expectations seem attainable and meaningful, teams feel self directed and intrinsically motivated. Progress flows from clarity.

The foundational step in expectation setting involves defining goals with exacting specificity:

- Set quantitative metrics: Include precise numerical objectives regarding revenues, costs, production targets, release dates, enrollment figures, or other quantifiable metrics.
- Set qualitative goals: Outline any qualitative dimensions like improving customer satisfaction scores, raising brand awareness by a certain percentage, reducing safety incidents, or achieving diversity benchmarks.
- Delineate deadlines: Attach definitive timeline milestones to each goal by which it must be completed. Deadlines crystallize urgency.
- Ensure attainability: Verify that expectations are realistic given available resources, personnel capabilities, and environmental constraints. Impossible goals demoralize.
- Allow input: Collaborate with teams to welcome their perspectives on goal formulation. Facilitate dialogue until alignment is reached.

Precise, timebound, and attainable goals provide clarity of purpose. Teams understand exactly what the targets are and when they must be accomplished. Without this foundation, efforts scatter.

Clarify Processes and Resources

In addition to goals, leaders must specify what resources teams will have available and what processes should guide their work:

- Outline workflow: Explain the step by step activities, sequencing, handoffs, and milestones expected to achieve the goals.
- Provide personnel: Ensure staffing levels, cross training, and external partnerships exist to facilitate requisite work volumes.
- Offer tools/technology: Confirm that teams have access to the tools, systems, equipment, and technical infrastructure needed for optimal execution.
- Enable training: Provide training opportunities to build any skills or knowledge gaps in relation to assigned goals.
- Allocate budgets: Appropriate sufficient budgets and decision autonomy so teams can acquire necessary materials and services within reason.

When expectations around operational factors are vague, people grow frustrated. Equip them thoroughly for success.

Define Individual Roles

The next layer of clarity involves each team member understanding their individual responsibilities:

- Delineate roles: Specify who will fulfill which duties in relation to the broader workflow and goals. Clear owners must exist for each domain.
- Outline authority: Make transparent the level of decision latitude and autonomy each role is afforded. Micromanagers breed dissatisfaction.
- Communicate team interdependencies: Illustrate how roles interconnected and rely on one another for seamless coordination.
- Allow role flexibility: Remain open to improving role clarity as unexpected needs arise. Teams close to the work may shift.

With roles undefined, gaps and redundancies materialize. People become tentative without direction. Eliminate ambiguity around responsibilities.

Track Progress Transparently

Leaders must establish clear metrics for gauging success:

- Select key performance indicators: Identify quantifiable and qualitative metrics that will serve as decision useful measures of progress toward goals.
- Automate tracking: Utilize digital dashboards and tracking tools rather than manual reports where possible. This provides real time visibility.

- Establish reporting routines: Institute regular progress review meetings, calls, or email updates to discuss metrics.
- Course correct quickly: If metrics lag, quickly diagnose root causes and develop countermeasures. Nip issues in the bud.
- Report failures transparently: When setbacks occur, avoid concealing them. Reveal shortfalls openly and reset expectations if warranted.

Defining how success will be evaluated and routinely reviewing metrics accelerates learning and improvement. Quickly identify what is working vs. what needs remediation. Transparency around progress builds trust.

Cultivate Ownership and Motivation

For expectations to truly take root, teams must feel invested, not just mandated. Foster collective ownership by:

- Explaining why goals matter: Illustrate how team and individual work ladders up to serve the organization's higher mission and purpose. Inspire with meaning.
- Encouraging participation: Solicit input and ideas from the team on how best to achieve the goals. This leads to greater creativity, commitment, and effort.

- Expressing confidence: Praise past shared accomplishments. Highlight current team strengths and talents that will enable success.
- Allowing autonomy: Within defined boundaries, provide discretion over how goals are met. Independence and trust breed engagement.

With clear expectations comes accountability. But coupling clarity with ownership propels teams to surpass what was thought possible, motivated by freedom and purpose.

Navigating Change

Although concrete expectations provide focus, leaders must remain flexible when conditions shift. As new challenges emerge, goals and timelines may require realignment. Keep expectations a dynamic dialogue, not rigid dogma.

Constantly reevaluate relevance as competitive threats evolve, new technologies emerge, economic forces fluctuate, or consumer preferences change. Periodically update goals and processes to keep pace.

Transparently explain the rationale for any major realignments to teams. Sudden unexplained shifts are jarring. Maintain consistency when possible, but adapt expectations when the situation demands it. Balance constancy with flexibility.

Set the Tone

Leaders set the tone for expectations. By dedicating time and care to formulating and communicating priorities with exactness, you enable your organization to thrive. Replace ambiguity with understanding. Foster accountability without micromanagement. Through clarity, unlock potential.

Chapter 6 Trust Your Team

An eternal question leaders face involves the appropriate level of autonomy to provide team members. While appropriate oversight is prudent, hypermanagement stifles initiative. Leaders must strike a delicate balance between direction and independence. Mastery entails giving your team wings to chart their own flight path within the context of broader organizational priorities.

Trust represents the foundation on which empowerment rests. Leaders who micromanage signal fundamental distrust in their people's capabilities and judgment. When trust is absent, handing over discretion backfires. However, leaders who cultivate faith in their team's competence through relationship building and evidence based confidence boosting can gradually expand autonomy as abilities grow.

Freedom catalyzes innovation and accountability. Given clear expectations by a trusting leader, teams often devise more effective solutions and feel greater ownership over outcomes. Empowerment concentrates purpose and responsibility. Rather than passive followers, engaged participants emerge.

Leaders sometimes struggle to loosen the reins and provide team members latitude. However, obsessive control has consequences:

- Stifled innovation: New ideas and process improvements get smothered when people lack discretion to try novel approaches. Status quo calcifies.
- Lack of ownership: "Just following orders" passivity replaces personal commitment to excellence. No one feels accountable.
- Helplessness: People lose confidence in their own judgment and problem solving capabilities when denied opportunity to exercise them.
- Disengagement: Micromanagement communicates lack of trust. This devalues team members' human need to feel respected and self directed.
- Bottlenecks: Every minor decision gets funneled upward, creating logjams. Progress halts awaiting leader directives.
- Burnout: When leaders become overwhelmed by excessive tactical details, higher order strategic priorities suffer. Energy drains.

While appropriate oversight has benefits, excessive control achieves the reverse. Empowered teams outperform constrained ones.

Develop a Trust Foundation

Expanding autonomy requires nurturing mutual trust between leader and team. Trust grows through:

- Results track record: Leaders gain credibility by demonstrating past collective success. Teams trust proven effectiveness.
- Relationship building: Invest time in understanding team members' needs, goals, and strengths on a personal level. Care builds loyalty.
- Vulnerability: Admit your own mistakes and limitations. Letting the "leader armor" down signals authenticity and builds trust.
- Delegation: Start small by delegating low risk tasks with clear expectations. As success follows, gradually expand responsibility.
- Two Way dialogue: Have candid discussions about interests, concerns, and expectations around empowerment. Air doubts transparently.
- Consistency: Build trust gradually by making empowerment an organizational habit, not a one off event. Reinforce it daily.

Leaders who rush to empower without cultivating psychological safety through trust find teams hesitant to fully embrace autonomy. Trust unlocks potential.

Expanding empowerment requires a phased approach aligned with team capabilities:

- Start small: Initially, provide latitude over lower risk, narrowly defined tasks and decisions. Success breeds confidence.
- Widen boundaries: As competencies grow, broaden the scope of authority and choice team members have over parameters like budgets, timelines, tools etc.
- Loosen supervision: Reduce control by requiring fewer approvals, status updates etc. Avoid micromanaging execution.
- Add responsibilities: Entrust additional complex tasks and decisions reflecting your growing confidence in their judgment.
- Inspire innovation: Encourage teams to try new strategies and make process improvements within guidelines. Welcome creativity.
- Address failures: When missteps inevitably happen under greater autonomy, avoid blame and instead provide guidance. Reframe setbacks as learning opportunities.

Rome wasn't built in a day. Steadily elevating empowerment allows people to get comfortable with enhanced discretion and accountability.

As a leader handing over greater control, you must shift from handson doer to architect and advisor:

- Set clear boundaries: Make goals, resources, constraints, and success metrics highly transparent. Establish guardrails for empowerment.
- Be a resource: Make yourself available to provide guidance, feedback, and coaching. Offer teams your expertise while letting them remain in the driver's seat.
- Guide values: While granting teams latitude over execution, reinforce overarching cultural values that set standards for behavior.
- Foster connections: Facilitate collaboration between teams by making cross functional introductions and building relationships. A well connected organization maximizes empowerment.

Your focus expands from tactics to culture and strategy. By empowering others, you amplify impact and develop future leaders.

Address Fear Factors

When delegating authority, many leaders self sabotage due to hidden fears:

- Loss of control: Relying on others feels precarious. Understand no leader truly works independently. You must build mutual trust.
- Aversion to conflict: Potential disagreements with empowered team members can be uncomfortable. However, constructive discord yields better solutions.
- Perfectionism: You may worry that delegated work won't meet your quality standards. But the growth opportunity outweighs short term roughness.
- Inadequacy fears: Do you secretly believe you are indispensable or that no one can perform tasks as well? The right team has untapped talents.

By naming these fears, their irrationality becomes clear. You must believe in people to empower them.

The Keys to Success

Done effectively, heightened autonomy breeds innovation, fulfillment, and ownership. As Simon Sinek says, "Employees will never fully care about your business until they feel you first care about them." Empowerment signals deep care and trust.

Handle missteps with empathy and patience. People may test boundaries at first. With supportive guidance, teams rise to meet empowerment with responsibility and achievement.

By lifting constraints and granting freedom, leaders transform passive teams into empowered participants dedicated to shared success. Your courage and trust enable greatness.

Chapter 7 Wield the Power of Influence

The capacity to influence others represents an indispensable instrument in a leader's toolkit. In diverse settings ranging from steering meetings, pitching ideas, negotiating agreements, or driving change, a leader's effectiveness hinges on their ability to gain willing buy-in and cooperation. Those lacking savvy to mobilize support for their vision struggle to advance goals. Mastering the nuances of high impact influence amplifies leadership reach.

Contrary to some misconceptions, influence does not equate to authoritarian strongarming, slick manipulation, or charisma. While such techniques may yield compliance short term, they fail to generate authentic commitment and may trigger resentment or resistance. Lasting influence relies on ethical use of psychology, reason, and relationship building skill.

By understanding people's core motivations and tailoring communications accordingly, leaders can frame requests persuasively. When rational analysis and empathy converge, influence flows naturally. Wield this power judiciously to serve your teams and mission. The higher the stakes, the greater the need for influence mastery.

Cultivate Credibility and Trustworthiness

People gravitate toward those perceived as credible and trustworthy. Leaders can build these perceptions through:

- Demonstrating expertise: Show depth of knowledge on key issues. Back statements with facts and details. Credibility grows when you prove competence.
- Achieving results: Influence expands through consistently delivering concrete results. Outcomes build reputations over time.
- Exhibiting integrity: Keep promises, own mistakes, and adhere to strong values. Reliability and ethics breed trust.
- Communicating respectfully: Avoid condescension, manipulation, or belittling language. Respect is dignified.
- Valuing all voices: Show willingness to listen to dissenting views non-defensively. Openness signals fairness and care.

Trust and credibility make people receptive when tough conversations arise. These qualities ultimately persuade more than charisma alone. They also make teams support ideas originating from others you empower.

Rather than resorting to hardball demands or threats, influential leaders align around mutually beneficial interests:

- Understand motivations: Ask insightful questions to discern the priorities, concerns, and goals of those you aim to persuade. What incentives guide them? Then identify overlapping interests.
- Make the ask a solution: Demonstrate how your request solves a problem or advances shared goals. Show it is in everyone's favor.
- Establish common ground: Before addressing differences, build rapport by first discussing areas of philosophical agreement and shared values. This primes openness.
- Leverage higher purpose: Inspiring leaders point toward "why" their request matters for the greater good. Shared ideals build unity.

With influence, cooperation beats coercion. Help people perceive alignment between your goals and their needs. Collaboration follows.

Back Words with Proof

For maximum sway, leaders must buttress verbal arguments with evidence:

- Provide precedent examples: Reference specific past successes that illustrate the validity of your request. Proven models are persuasive.
- Offer logical reasoning: Break down the rationale step by step. Airtight logic convinces skeptics.
- Cite data/statistics: Numbers, metrics, surveys, and other hard data boost objectivity. Facts counteract subjectivity.
- Obtain expert endorsement: Have respected third parties affirm your position. External validation lends credence.
- Provide a cost/benefit analysis: Quantify both the investment required and the expected return. Demonstrate compelling value.

When words sync with demonstrable proof points, arguments become irrefutable. Give substance to statements.

Effective influencers adapt their style to each unique audience:

- Match communication modes: Some gravitate toward data, others need big picture vision. Tailor to their preference.
- Gauge emotional state: If someone seems closed off, impatient or upset, address that first. Emotions impact receptivity.
- Understand personalities: What persuades a dominant extrovert differs from a cautious introvert. Factor in temperament.
- Consider backgrounds: People from different cultures or professions appreciate varied approaches. Context matters.
- Read body language: Note nonverbal cues that signal disagreement or resistance. Pause and reframe if needed.

Just as there is no one size fits all approach to leadership overall, influence requires personalization and situational awareness to resonate maximally. Internalize this, and your powers of persuasion expand exponentially.

With enhanced influence comes greater obligation to wield it responsibly. Avoid these pitfalls:

- Manipulation or coercion: Do not intimidate or impose your will on people. Pressure contradicts consent.
- Optics over substance: Flashy presentations without factual depth sabotage long term trust. Prioritize truth.
- Conflicts of interest: Never exploit influence for personal gain at the expense of others. This constitutes abuse.
- Inflexibility: Influence does not necessitate dogmatic adherence to initial stances. Compromise may become necessary.
- Chronic resistance: If someone truly cannot be influenced despite exhaustive efforts, continuing attempts become harassment. Respect boundaries.

Leaders with integrity promote transparency, remain open to counter perspectives, and focus on serving people over themselves. Principled influence uplifts.

The Capacity to Change Minds

In summary, when wielded ethically and backed by credibility, rationality and care, a leader's power to influence opinion, inspire teams and drive change expands exponentially. But it requires patience, self awareness, and dedication to rapport building. Earn influence step by step, and you gain a potent capacity to shape hearts, minds and communities for the better.

Though influence rests on intangible factors like trust and rapport, its impact leads to very tangible results. Invest in mastering this subtle art, and your leadership knows no bounds. Plant seeds of change through empowering influence…

Chapter 8 Adapt Your Leadership Style

An effective leadership style recognizes that diverse personalities require tailored guidance approaches. While standardized systems have benefits, human dynamics necessitate a degree of flexibility. Astute leaders adapt their methods to optimize the fit between their innate preferences and those on the receiving end. Rather than demanding people adapt to you, customize your style to bring out their best.

This versatility enables you to motivate people across the spectrum, from outspoken extraverts requiring empowerment to cautious introverts needing reassurance. Adapting your communication, feedback delivery, and coaching to align with individuals' work styles and temperaments breeds engagement and development.

No cookiecutter formula exists. Each team member represents a unique combination of personality, motivations, strengths, and growth areas. Continually strive to understand these nuances, and refine your techniques accordingly. Lead the person, not the role description.

Expanding your leadership repertoire involves:

- Communication modes: Adjust between high level themes, detailed analysis, visual aids, and interpersonal dynamics depending on preferences.
- Feedback strategies: Some respond better to direct critiques, others need indirect guidance. Consider sensitivity levels.
- Recognition approaches: Public praise motivates some personalities, private acknowledgement inspires others. Cater accordingly.
- Goal Setting: Those needing structure appreciate defined objectives and key results. Free spirits chafe under rigidity.
- Coaching methods: Socratic questioning unearths solutions for analytical types. But directive advice provides clarity for linear thinkers.
- Meeting facilitation: Engage extroverts actively but create space for introverts' input. Balance participation styles.

Avoid a rigid mindset that one style fits all scenarios. Expand your capabilities through the range.

Understand Personality Styles

Gaining insights into team members' personality styles and workplace behaviors enables you to tailor leadership approaches. Useful frameworks include:

- MyersBriggs: classifies people across spectrums like introversion/extroversion, thinking/feeling.
- DISC: focuses on traits like dominance, influence, steadiness, compliance.
- Enneagram: identifies 9 personality types, like achiever, investigator, enthusiast.

While imperfect, these models offer helpful mental frameworks to categorize tendencies, preferences, motivations etc. Integrate insights from them into your influence strategy.

Get to Know Your Team

More valuable than test results are direct observations and conversations to form intuitive understandings of what makes each person tick:

- Notice work habits: Is the person methodical or spontaneous? Do they prefer set routines or freedom? Observe tendencies.
- Gauge background: How might their education, cultural norms, and past roles shape preferences? Consider context.
- Discuss expectations openly: Ask what guidance approach resonates most. Invite candid input.

- Test different styles: Experiment by, for example, giving more praise to one person and more constructive criticism to another. See what lands best.
- Check In regularly: Proactively ask for feedback on how your leadership style impacts them. Incorporate lessons.

Making inferences is useful but risks misjudgments. Talk openly to confirm theories. Curiosity deepens bonds.

Lead as Your Best Self

Adapting does not require abandoning your natural inclinations. The most effective shapeshifting leaders flex their approach while staying true to their core selves:

- Know your tendencies: Being self-aware of inherent style allows you to compensate elsewhere.
- Double down on strengths: While stretching beyond comfort zones, lean prominently on innate gifts so you avoid inauthenticity.
- Don't betray values: Remain thoughtful and ethical when responding to different preferences.
- Seek integration: Blend insights gained from various frameworks into your unique leadership identity. Build on your philosophy.

- Keep developing self: Exploring flexible behaviors builds emotional intelligence and relationships. But stay grounded in who you are.

Growth occurs by working with not against your nature. Let versatility accentuate your distinct leadership talents.

Adaptability Mindsets

Cultivating versatility requires adopting growth mindsets:

- Accept imperfection: You will never tailor leadership perfectly for every individual. Effort matters most.
- Embrace discomfort: Operating outside natural preferences feels awkward initially. Persist through learning anxiety.
- Relish diversity: See variation between people as an asset, not a hassle. It makes interactions more colorful.
- Remain patient: People's needs may not always be immediately clear. Peel the onion over multiple interactions.
- Expect surprises: Just when you feel someone figured out, new dimensions may emerge. Drop fixed assumptions.
- Remember context: Correct style aligns not just with personality but also role, tenure, project phase, business conditions etc.

Stay perpetually curious. You can always expand your understanding of how to inspire the rich spectrum of personalities around you.

By dedicating yourself to understanding the complexities of human dynamics, you become an increasingly rare leader, one who truly sees, supports, and brings out the best in people. Make it your life's work.

Chapter 9 Stop the Bullshit - Giving Candid Feedback

Within leadership, delivering candid feedback represents a high leverage yet avoided responsibility. While praise feels more comfortable, critique provokes growth. Tactful candor illuminates blind spots and motivates improvement. However, many leaders sugarcoat negative feedback or avoid it entirely to dodge interpersonal discomfort. This does a disservice to team members striving for excellence.

Outstanding leaders recognize candid feedback as a gift to be valued, not confrontation to be dodged. They critique with care, emphasizing growth opportunities rather than deficiencies. Their respectful honesty strengthens relationships rooted in trust. Team members know where they stand and understand areas needing refinement to maximize impact.

Delivering excellent feedback requires courage, empathy and skill. Leaders must critique with nuance, situationally adapt their approach, listen to reactions non defensively, and inspire action plans. Unlocking people's potential necessitates candid feedback, as long as the intent remains supportive.

Masterful feedback adheres to core principles:

- Situationally relevant: Tie observations directly to recent, tangible examples. Don't rely on vague generalities.
- Actionable: Focus on behaviors within one's control. Avoid critiquing inherent personality traits.
- Balanced: Address strengths alongside areas for improvement. Praise existing competencies.
- Twoway: Invite reciprocal feedback on your own leadership. This models openness.
- Future focused: Emphasize growth opportunities ahead rather than past mistakes. Take a forward looking mindset.
- Specific: Cite precise behaviors to continue or change. Generalizations cause confusion.
- Kind: Critique the action, not the person. Respect demonstrates care.

Feedback rooted in real examples, focused on growth, delivered with care unleashes potential.

When providing feedback, adapt your approach to the individual:

- Personality factors: More resilient personalities can handle blunt directness. Tactful indirectness suits sensitive individuals. Adjust accordingly.
- Culture/background: Certain cultures prize indirect feedback. Others respect directness. Contextual awareness prevents miscommunications.
- Feedback history: If there is limited existing rapport, begin with "feedback sandwiches" where critiques are cushioned between praise. Once a relationship deepens, you can pivot to provide more direct feedback.
- Opportunity timing: If possible, schedule feedback conversations separate from project demands, when the person can focus solely on absorbing insights.

No one size fits all approach exists. Tailor timing, mode, and language to the person while upholding consistency.

Listen Actively to Reactions

Once negative feedback is given, leaders must intently listen to reactions without instinctive defensiveness:

- Allow processing time: After sharing critique, provide space for people to voice reactions before problem solving together.
- Ask probing questions: Inquire into any confusion or hurt. Seek to deeply understand their viewpoint.
- Paraphrase responses: Restate what you hear in your own words. This confirms you comprehend emotions behind statements.
- Apologize if appropriate: If your feedback delivery missed the mark, own the mistake sincerely. Make amends.
- Find truth in dissent: Even if you disagree with their assessment of the feedback, look for valid insights you may have missed.
- Letting people feel fully heard deepens trust and constructive dialogue. Avoid glossing over negative reactions. Work through them.

The final step entails collaboratively building action plans:

- Find common ground: Establish shared goals and desired outcomes. Align on hope for their development.
- Solicit solutions: Ask "What steps do you think could address these growth areas effectively?" Empower their ideas.
- Offer resources: Provide training opportunities, mentors, and other support systems to help fulfill plans.
- Define milestones: Outline measurable markers of success to track progress over time.
- Schedule follow ups: Book future one on one meetings to discuss wins, challenges etc. Continuity drives change.
- Check emotional state: Before concluding, assess their readiness to immediately reengage with responsibilities. Adjust if emotions remain raw.

Great feedback conversations spark motivation and movement. People leave with clarity, support, and renewed purpose.

Develop a TrustBased Culture

For feedback to truly take root across an organization, leaders must nurture a hightrust culture:

- Model vulnerability: Admit your own errors and developmental areas first. This empowers reciprocity.
- Reward growth efforts: Applaud good faith attempts to implement feedback, even if outcomes are imperfect. Recognize courage.
- Normalize candidness: Institute regular touchpoints for open dialogue free of repercussions. Safe environments breed transparency.
- Discourage sugarcoating: Challenge tendencies toward vague, inflated praise that inhibits growth.
- Define feedback guidelines: Cocreate ground rules upholding psychologically safe boundaries and kindness.
- With organizational habits and norms that cherish truth telling, teams learn to both give and receive feedback gracefully.

Delivering excellent feedback requires compassion, acumen and tenacity. But when leaders invest wholeheartedly in this work, people blossom in wondrous ways. Uncomfortable conversations transform into fulfilling growth journeys that unlock potential and strengthen bonds.

Make it your purpose as a leader to have people leave conversations understanding exactly where they excel and where they have room to grow. Match candor with care. By embracing courageous feedback, you ignite the spark of excellence.

Chapter 10 Encourage Feedback from Others

Exemplary leaders recognize that seeking frequent feedback represents a cornerstone of their own growth and effectiveness. Rather than avoiding criticism, outstanding leaders actively solicit input from colleagues, mentors, and even direct reports to illuminate blind spots and refine their approach. They embrace feedback courageously, even when it stings, understanding its gifts outweigh short term discomfort.

This thirst for input and accountability separates exceptional leaders from mediocre ones. Developing robust feedback channels both formally and informally fosters continual improvement at all levels of an organization. As leaders model openness to critiques of their own performance, it establishes norms for others.

The question is not if you will receive feedback as a leader, but rather how well you confront it. Feedback may arrive loudly through formal surveys or subtle whispers in the hallway. But for those focused on excellence, even small signals offer valuable insight. Be eager to not just give feedback, but also receive it.

Expanding your comfort with feedback begins with mindset shifts:

- Seek truth over validation: Orient toward constructive criticism rather than fishing for praise and confirmation.
- Focus on growth not judgment: View feedback as indispensable data for your evolution rather than a fixed evaluation of your worthiness.
- Embrace productive discomfort: Hearing difficult truths often sparks initial defensiveness. But push past knee jerk reactions to find value.
- Adopt a learner mentality: Maintain insatiable curiosity about how you can refine your leadership. Feedback provides clues.
- Remember imperfection: As humans, we all have room for improvement. Feedback merely illuminates areas ready for enhancement.

If you approach feedback opportunities with a receptive, growth focused mentality, you gain invaluable insight. Let go of false notions that constructive input diminishes your value.

In addition to an open mindset, leaders need concrete systems to elicit formal feedback:

- Leadership reviews: Institute annual or biannual reviews where managers, peers, and direct reports offer anonymous input on your effectiveness.
- Surveys: Send quarterly questionnaires asking for ratings and comments on your communication, vision, empowerment, etc.
- Suggestion channels: Create centralized online systems for submitting confidential feedback about any leader's performance.
- Town halls: Use skip level meetings to hear unfiltered perspectives from lower levels that fosters candid dialogue.
- External input: Request leadership coaching, join peer advisory groups, or complete 360 reviews to gain outside observer feedback.
- Performance metrics: Track indicators like team productivity, satisfaction, turnover etc. for clues on where leadership falls short.

By proactively seeking formal feedback via these channels, you take responsibility for your own development rather than waiting passively.

Cultivate Informal Feedback Channels

Alongside formal systems, optimize informal feedback opportunities:

- Ask directly: After meetings, projects, presentations etc., request quick candid reactions on what went well or could improve. Make asking habitual.
- Remove barriers: Foster psychological safety by ensuring no one faces repercussions for critiquing your leadership respectfully.
- Share your requests: Make it broadly known that you welcome candid feedback from anyone. Circulate contact options.
- Probe issues: Dig into disagreements, conflicts, and resignations to uncover leadership related factors you could improve.
- Watch for cues: Note body language, tone, and indirect behaviors that may signal discomfort with your leadership approach. Explore.

- Debrief mistakes: When errors happen, discuss contributing leadership factors. The best learning follows failure.

Daily interactions offer rich chances to gather feedback if you remain attentive. Capture these fleeting opportunities.

Respond to Feedback Gracefully

When receiving criticism, strive to:

- Listen fully before reacting: Hear people out without instinctive defensiveness. Allow silence to soak in main points.
- Clarify details: Ask follow up questions to deepen understanding rather than dismissing blanket statements. Get granular.
- Find truth in errors: Even if feedback seems biased or delivered poorly, look forvalidity within imperfections. Extract learning.
- Express gratitude: Thank the person sincerely for caring enough to share candid reactions. This encourages future transparency.
- Outline action steps: Verbalize how you plan to digest and apply the feedback. Articulating next steps provides closure.

Modeling poise and appreciation when facing criticism, even if unfairly delivered, speaks volumes about your leadership.

Feedback only nourishes growth if acted upon:

- Reflect before deciding: Avoid knee jerk reactions to feedback. Take time to discern appropriate next steps.
- Prioritize high impact areas: Focus your initial improvement efforts on feedback themes appearing repeatedly from multiple sources.
- Start small: Break large development areas into incremental changes for gradual improvement over time.
- Update stakeholders: Let those who provided feedback know what steps you will take to address it. Follow through reliably.
- Monitor progress: After making adjustments, solicit candid reactions on whether the desired changes have manifested.
- Get coaching: If struggling to implement changes alone, don't hesitate to enlist leadership coaches or mentors for support.

With strategic followthrough, feedback leads to measurable enhancement. Let evidence affirm you are translating insights into positive change.

Model Feedback Thirst Organizationally

As feedback loops enrich your leadership, champion them organization wide:

- Spotlight exemplars: Publicly praise leaders who actively seek critical feedback and implement improvements. This establishes desired norms.
- Address resistance: If some remain closed off to feedback, conduct coaching to overcome defensive mindsets.
- Train supervisors: Provide managers training to deliver excellent feedback and cultivate trusting relationships where candidness thrives.
- Revise systems: Ensure performance management and survey systems focus on enriching feedback over rigid evaluation.
- Thank challengers: Express gratitude to truth tellers. Make it safe to constructively critique anyone without vindictiveness.
- Address politics: Where office politics hinder honest feedback, tackle issues

transparently. Safe environments allow people to focus on meaningful growth.

By weaving a feedback positive culture, you multiply leadership improvement across every level of the organization.

Offering and receiving honest feedback requires courage, imperfect as the process may be. However, leaders shaped and sharpened through transparency, input, and accountability gain capabilities beyond those who surround themselves with confirmation and accolades.

If you aspire to become the best leader possible in service of your teams, be voracious for feedback in all its forms.

- *Lean into discomfort.*
- *Let go of your ego.*

The wisdom you gain will far outweigh temporary unease. Emerge wiser, more self aware and more impactful. Feedback charts the path to excellence.

Conclusion

The journey to becoming an exceptional leader is a lifelong endeavor filled with challenge and reward. By committing to continuously expanding your capabilities, you position yourself to unlock untapped potential within your teams, organization, and yourself.

Through this book, we have explored the hallmarks of influential leadership across critical domains – from igniting enthusiasm to delivering candid feedback. Mastering these leadership skills produces a multiplying effect, elevating your impact across the board.

While absorbing insights is valuable, true development requires translating knowledge into action. Review the strategies presented, reflect on opportunities for growth, and purposefully hone the areas that will help you and your teams thrive. Set an ambitious vision for your leadership, and then take it step by step.

Remember that leadership is not a solo sport. Surround yourself with mentors and peers who can provide guidance, accountability and encouragement along the journey. Stay hungry for feedback and self improvement. By investing yourself in lifelong betterment, your capabilities will continue rising to meet the ever increasing challenges you face.

Leadership ultimately comes down to serving people. Strive each day to understand individuals more deeply, uplift them and unlock their potential. Lead with compassion, integrity and an insatiable commitment to excellence.

I hope the concepts and techniques offered in this book provide fuel to ignite your leadership growth. Absorb what resonates, modify what needs adaptation to your situation, and discard what rings untrue. Chart your own path.

Believe in your growing ability to positively influence others and spearhead change. Leadership is a noble calling. Pursue it wholeheartedly, and leave behind a meaningful legacy. I wish you the very best.